Rugby Lads Local

"The shortest
word for me is I,
the sweetest word
for me is LOVE,
but the only word
for me is Rugby"

FRANCE

TOP16-PROD2

FORCE XV

7

Adecco

aruVendu
ParuVen

Proact
A.S.B
VAUCLUSE
ParuVendu

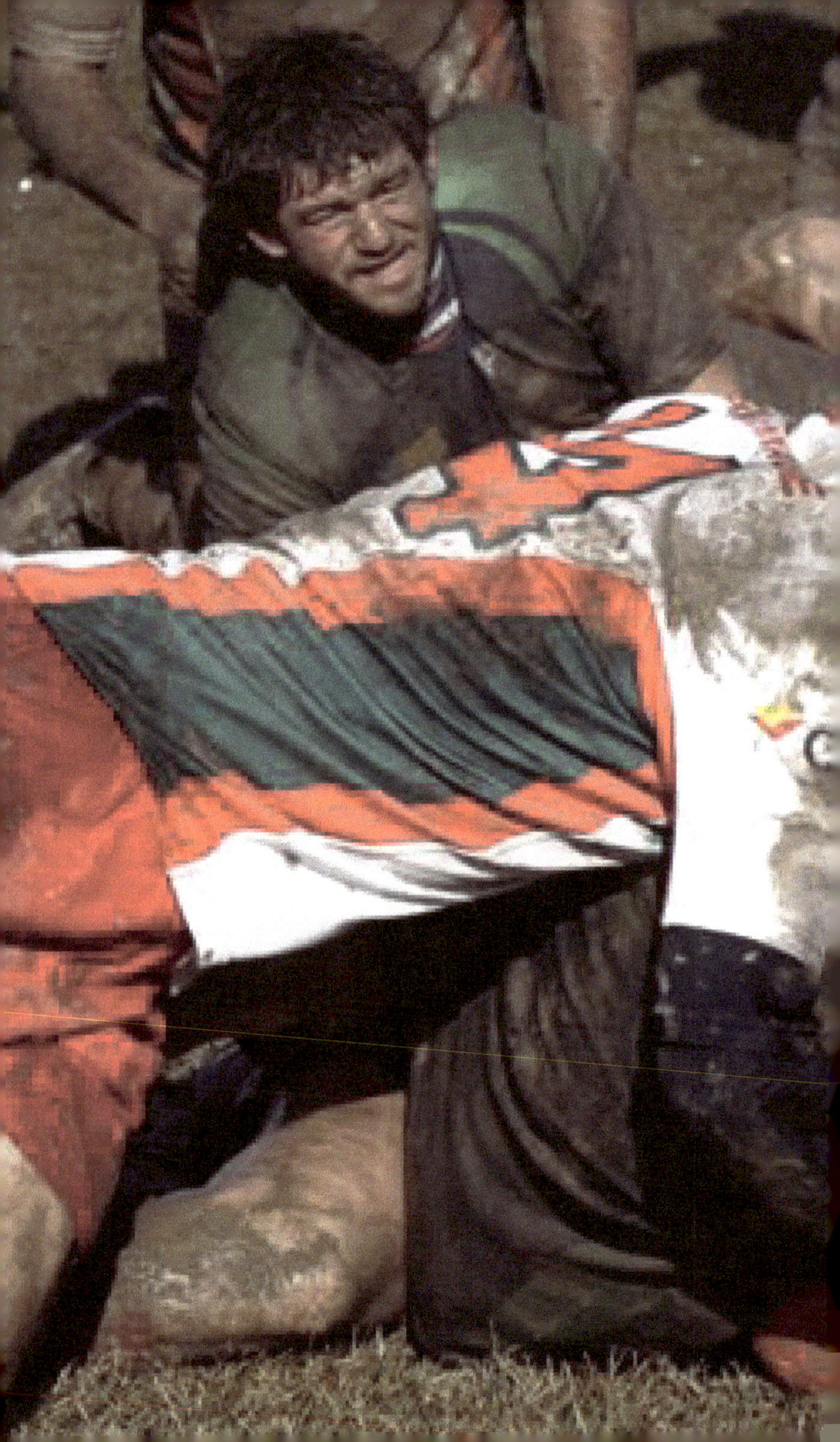

Vendu
Vendu

JD'AI
Aux DOCKS du BUREAU
Tous mobiliers de bureau
TEISSEIRE
CUISINES & BAINS

Martignon Pneus
Pneus
Vidange
éométrie
Freins
Coca-Cola
Alain
TEISSEIRE
CUISINES & BAINS
CUISINE TEISSEIRE

73

10

McDonald's
FACE PLACE
DE LA
REVOLUTION
BLAGNAC
7J/7
AIRBUS
JD'AI
Aux DOCKS
orange
Les Jardins
Toulousains
TEISSEIRE

ISO MAT
spirit
Maeva
GTM
AKERYS
TEISSEIRE
LA DEPECHE

10

CLUB
Perrier

1 195

195

NSD
INTERMARCHÉ

BRICOLAGE
VILLE

CPSIA information can be obtained
at www.ICGtesting.com
Printed in the USA
BVHW090824290719
554567BV00024B/1680/P

9 780464 089148